DEDICATION

To my magnificent mom, Mary Christian, who transcended in 2012. To all the ancestors, family, and friends who paved the way for me to make this book possible – I Thank You!

ASE! 729.

Balboa Press books may be ordered through booksellers or by contacting:

Balboa Press
A Division of Hay House
1663 Liberty Drive
Bloomington, IN 47403
www.balboapress.com
1 (877) 407-4847

Because of the dynamic nature of the Internet, any web addresses or links contained in this book may have changed since publication and may no longer be valid. The views expressed in this work are solely those of the author and do not necessarily reflect the views of the publisher, and the publisher hereby disclaims any responsibility for them.

ISBN: 978-1-9822-3283-2 (sc)
ISBN: 978-1-9822-3282-5 (e)

Library of Congress Control Number: 2019911588

Print information available on the last page.

Balboa Press rev. date: 11/06/2019

BALBOA
PRESS
A DIVISION OF HAY HOUSE

Talking
to the
HERBS & CRYSTALS TOO!

Liz Christian

CONTENTS

Dedication iii

Introduction ix

Chapter 1 Gut Health (Root Chakra) 1

   Herbs For Colon Cleansing: 2

      Black Walnut Husk 2

      Rhubarb Root 2

   Crystals For Healing: 3

      Bloodstone 3

      Garnet 3

      Red Jasper 3

Chapter 2 Urinary, Reproductive, Sexual Health (Sacral Chakra) 5

   Herbs For Healing: 5

      Black Cohosh 5

      Blue Cohosh 6

      Capadulla 6

      Catuaba 6

      Chasteberry 6

      Cramp Bark 7

      Damiana 7

      Muira Puama Root 7

      Shepherds Purse 7

      Irish Sea Moss 8

      Stinging Nettle 9

   Crystals For Healing: 9

      Moonstone 9

      Carnelian 9

      Pearl Abalone 10

      Calcite (Orange) 10

      Citrine 10

      Zincite 10

Chapter 3 Digestive Skin Health (Solar Plexus Chakra) 11

   Herbs For Healing: 11

      Burdock Root 11

      Cayenne Pepper 12

      Comfrey 12

      Red Clover 13

      Sarsaparilla 13

      Yellow Dock 13

   Crystals For Healing: 14

      Amber 14

      Citrine 14

      Copper 14

Chapter 4 Blood, Cardiovascular, Respiratory/Chest Health (Heart Chakra) 15

   Herbs For Healing: 15

      Chaparral 15

      Lilly of the Valley 15

      Motherwort 16

      Milk Thistle 16

      Prickly Ash Bark 16

      Yellow Dock 16

   Crystals For Healing: 17

      Aventurine 17

      Jade 17

      Malachite 17

      Rose Quartz 17

      Rose Water Mist 18

Chapter 5 Throat & Gland Health (Throat Chakra) 19

   Herbs For Healing: 19

      Bladderwrack 19

      Cleavers 19

      Elderberry 20

      DIY Elderberry Cough Syrup 20

Chapter 6 Ears, Vision, Neurological Disorders Health (Brow Chakra) 21

   Herbs For Healing: 21

      Eyebright 21

      Kava Kava 22

      Pennywort 22

      Red Sage 22

      Chamomile 22

   Crystals For Healing: 23

      Angelite 23

      Lapis 23

      Sodalite 23

      Turquoise 23

Chapter 7 Emotional, Mental, Neurological Health (Crown Chakra) 25

    Herbs For Healing: 25

        Jamaican Dogwood 25

        Kava Kava Root 25

        Kola Nut...25

        Lady Slipper 26

        Lavender..26

        Lemon Balm 26

        Passion Flower 26

        Blue Vervain 26

    Crystals For Healing: 27

        Agate Purple 27

        Amethyst 27

        Lepidolite 27

        Sugilite..27

About the Author...29

INTRODUCTION

Herbs, minerals, and crystals are all natural occurring elements. Herbs and crystals have matter or energy tuned into the universe, used for healing. Their healing power transcends the physical and reaches the emotional, mental, and spiritual parts of us. Herbs and crystals have a direct effect on our chakras. You may ask, 'what are chakras?' Chakras are electric energy centers represented by colors in our body and flow from the top of our heads to the bottom of our feet. These energy centers regulate everything from organs, blood, and even our immune system, and can have a direct effect on our psyche. Here in this book, I have compiled some of my favorite herbs and crystals for your enjoyment. These herbs and crystals are beneficial to our vitality as humans with elements that aren't man made and proven beneficial to our life in order to thrive. It's time we get to the ROOT CAUSE of all kinds of diseases (dis-ease) rather than focusing on symptoms. Let's heal our bodies instead of masking the symptoms to make it easy for us to tolerate the unfavorable conditions that come with the disease! Disease cannot thrive when optimal alkaline conditions inside the body are met fully. Alkalinity rids the body of mucus allowing the body to heal.

"The herbs are for the healing of the nations"
- Revelations 22:2

"And God said, Behold, I have given you every herb bearing seed,
which is upon the face of all the earth, and every tree, in the which is
the fruit of a tree yielding seed; to you it shall be for meat."
- Genesis 1:29

CHAPTER 1
GUT HEALTH
(ROOT CHAKRA)

Our excretory system as humans, plays a major role in how we nourish our body, cells, blood, and organs. Think of it as our body "SEWER SYSTEM." The process of eliminating or detoxing byproducts begins here. Otherwise known as the 'root chakra' is a RED orb of electric energy that's located at the base of the spine situated between the anus and genital area. Sluggish or stagnate energy is held in the digestive tract, skin, liver, lymphatic system, reproductive system and kidney. This is also where hard core addictive behaviors are held. The behaviors range from narcotics, to gambling, food addiction, guilty pleasures, sexual pleasures, struggles, fear, hate, anger, resentment, depression, suicidal tendencies and general inability to "KEEP IT TOGETHER"! People may also experience stomach problems, rectal colon cancer, hemorrhoids, obesity, diarrhea, constipation. Show me a mad, angry, pitiful, can't stand to be around them person and I'll show you a person full of SHIT! LITERALLY! The first step of healing is to cleanse our colon through the detoxification process. We need this first before we look to remedy or heal any kind of disease. Our senses of security, survival, stability, and pleasures are all found in the root chakra or base chakra. Our disposal and reproductive system is also located in this region that's represented by an orb of red energy located at the bottom of the pelvis, base of the spine, or between anus and sexual organs. This is where we get our foundation or support for life. Some examples of root chakra imbalances that may occur in this region include financial issues, hunger, lack of food, suicide and sexuality.

IF YOU CAN'T GET A DATE IT'S PROBABLY SOMETHING YOU ATE!

Bitter Melon(Momordica charantia)- aid inside digestion by promoting flow of gastric juices and bile secretion. It also improves circulation promoting hair growth and nourished cells. Bitter melon has antioxidant properties that make it an excellent source of immune support and strength. It's anticancer properties help to fight tumor growth and nourish cells.

Black Walnut Hull (Juglans nigra): As super food found to prevent Candida. It is just as effective as commercial antifungal products. Black Walnut Husk is an ingredient found in countless over the counter products. Its anti-parasitic property is useful for treatment of intestinal parasites such as hookworms, pinworms, and tapeworms. it's useful for treating skin conditions, excess sweats, and digestive issues.

Cascara Sagrada (Rhamnus Purshiana): AKA Sacred Bark herb is harvested from West American trees. It is considered as a sacred bark, introduced to the Spanish by native Americans to cause relief from constipation. It's a purgative that's useful for treating chronic constipation and also a stimulant laxative, that's good for the digestive system. The herb can be used as a bitter tonic. It has the ability to aid peristalsis pushing matter forward leading to easy disposal of harmful waste toxins from the colon. The bark contains anthraquinones that give it the action laxatives use to promote a healthy clean colon. It's found in over the counter medications and combines well with licorice.

Chickweed (Stellaria media)- used as a tea or decoction is popularly known for appetite suppression. It soothes the digestive tract, decreases hunger pangs, relieves gas and bloating. It's full of vitamins and minerals such as vitamins A, B, &C that make it a great appetite suppressant. It's normally loaded with copper and can be used for treating skin conditions, cleanses, nourish and purifies the blood. Chickweed is good for giving relief to inflammation of the joints.

Rhubarb Root (Rheum Palmatum): It's commonly harvested in Turkey and China. Chinese refer to its root as "da huang." It has a purgative effect, and antiseptic astringent properties that make it good for assisting digestion. It's also effective at cleansing the colon of waste toxins to give you a clean healthy colon. In addition, it can be useful for reducing fever, relieving thirst and curing excessive sweating, menstrual problems, and skin conditions.

Wormwood(Artemisia absinthium): AKA mugwort, it's a bitter tonic with anthelmintic and anti-inflammatory properties. As in the name 'wormwood', it is a powerful anti-parasitic and anti-tumor herb used for treatment of pinworms, roundworms and tapeworms infections. It also reduces fever and destroys cancer cells, it's thought to kill 98% of cancer cells in 16 hours! Humans, livestock, and even the foods we eat are all subjected to harmful organisms and wormwood can be a safe natural way to eliminate intestinal invaders. Wormwood as a good source of antioxidants supports gallbladder and liver function.

CRYSTALS FOR HEALING:

Bloodstone: It dispels negative energy grounds and centers the body in its entirety. Bloodstone give healing energy that boost the immune system, nourish, detoxify and purify organs that are rich in blood such as intestines, kidneys, liver and spleen by reducing mucus in the body. It revitalizes and alkalizes the body promoting better circulation, and cures gut related issues. Bloodstone is an excellent grounding stone. It helps in relieving anger, aggression, irritability and sluggishness.

Garnet: It energizes, revitalizes, and brings balance to the root chakra. Garnet stimulates blood flow to the liver and relieves hemorrhage. It also promotes courage, stamina both physical and sexual. Good anchoring stone to stay grounded in truth and focus on dreams and other desires. Folklore thought garnet to provide light on Noah's ark.

Red Jasper: Red Jasper promotes grounded energy by keeping you balanced and tune to earth's energy. It enhances dreams, truth and sexual energy. red Jasper can help support our life force or "chi" energetic fields and blood circulation of the liver while promoting detoxification. It also helps to dissolve blockages in the body and ducts. Due to Red Jaspers mineral content it can be used as an elixir.

CHAPTER 2
URINARY, REPRODUCTIVE, SEXUAL HEALTH (SACRAL CHAKRA)

Our expressions, sexuality, and how we relate to other people is located in our sacral chakra. Also located here is our lower digestive system where we get nourishment and food absorption. You will find the sacral chakra represented by an orb of ORANGE electric energy that's located right below the belly, sometimes called the sexual chakra. Relationship and nurturing energy is stored right here as well. The feeling you get that sexual touch feels wrong, unclean, or unworthiness is here. Our intuitive energy is stored here, hence our fight or flight senses too. In this region is where your gut feeling that 'something isn't right' originates from. Also located here is your sexuality, that leads to relationships ("what do you have to offer"? "What do you bring to the table"?). It's also in this region that reproductive issues, menstrual issues, pre-menstrual issues, menopause, peri menopause, fibroids, prostate, testicular issues, impotency, stomach problems, intestines, spleen, kidney issues, and urinary issues are all held. Ladies this is where your yoni expression is found! IF YOU CAN'T GET IT UP CLEAN THE GUT!

HERBS FOR HEALING:

Black Cohosh (Cimicifuga racemosa): This herb is an alternative that's antispasmodic. Chinese and Native Americans most commonly use it for relaxing and stabilizing the female reproductive system by addressing hot flashes, night sweats, painful ovulation and menstrual pain. It's also great for reducing woman related tension and stress due to premenstrual syndrome (PMS). It helps to restore menstrual cycle in absence of it. Black Cohosh is found in over the counter medications that treat these kind of conditions. it can help induce labor, and balances hormones in men and women. It cures sexual dysfunction and stabilizes estrogen to increase fertility in women. It's also used in estrogen replacement therapy. Black Cohosh is quite different from Blue Cohosh. Do not self-prescribe Black Cohosh during pregnancy consult herbalist and or midwife.

Blue Cohosh (caulophyllum thalictroides): It's an antispasmodic and anti-rheumatic, uterine tonic. Known by the Native Americans as Papoose root, it has the ability to Tone and strengthen the uterus. It reduces false labor pains and eases the birthing process. Blue cohosh is useful for averting imminent miscarriage. It's helpful in treatment of delayed menstrual. It's also used by The Iroquois for joint pain and inflammation due to its anti-rheumatic properties. You should note however do not self-prescribe Blue Cohosh during pregnancy. Always consult an herbalist or midwife. Blue Cohosh can induce premature contractions resulting in abortion or miscarriage. So it's advised that you use in last week of pregnancy only under herbalist, midwife or doctor's advice.

Capadulla: Is a tonic, aphrodisiac and the useful part is the bark. It's as effective as Viagra in the treatment of erectile dysfunction (ED). Thought to be a key ingredient in making of Viagra and has zero side effects! It's a natural aphrodisiac that can also be referred to as bush medicine remedy for ED. To prepare it, boil the root until water turns red and drink as a tea concoction. Other names for Capdulla are (Doliocarpus major and Dalleniaceae).

Catuaba (juniperus brasiliensis): The useful parts of this herb are the bark and root. Catuaba is derived from the same family of plants that produces cocaine, but lacks the narcotic components. it is known in Brazil as an aphrodisiac and highly regarded by the Tupi people for its increased sexual arousal properties. it has the ability to increase sexual dreams and increase ability to maintain erections. In addition, it's useful for treating mental fatigue, memory-loss, and agitation. It is used as an elixir and sold as wine. Historically, it has been used by Brazilians to calm nerves, increase memory and treat nervous system.

Chasteberry (Vitex agnus-castus): As its name suggest, it helps with chastity by lowering or reducing the libido. it's useful for treating premenstrual syndrome (PMS), breast pain, painful menstrual flow and menopause symptoms. This herb has properties that balances sex hormone in females. It contains testosterone for curing erectile dysfunction(ED) treatment, swollen testicles, prostate issues and other male related sexual disorders. Chasteberry helps in treating acne monthly breakouts in chin areas by leveling hormones reducing PMS related acne. It helps to increase fertility in women and help reduce uterine fibroids by balancing hormone levels. Chasteberry helps balance progesterone and estrogen levels by bring the body towards balance.

Cramp Bark (Viburnum opulus): Parts used – bark, and sometimes berries. It has anti-spasmodic, astringent and sedative properties. As in the name, Cramp bark can be useful for cramps, chronic pain, muscle spasms, and muscle tension. It's also useful for treating ovarian and uterus cramps or when miscarriage is threatened. It's useful for menorrhagia or excessive prolonged bleeding during menstrual cycle. In addition, it's used for relieving kidney related pain due to kidney stones and urinary pain. Mixes well with Valerian.

Damiana (Turnera aphrodisiaca): It increases libido in men and women. It stimulates, nourishes and regulates hormones in men and women, strengthens the nervous system and blood circulation. It's also good for relieving mild depression, anxiety, menopause issues and decreases erectile dysfunction (ED) with good anti-inflammatory properties. A Power herb for women, it does a good job of reducing PMS symptoms such as  headaches, depression, pain, muscle pain and lower back pain. It reduces bedwetting, increases sexual performance, also useful for vaginal health when steaming... tighten, tones, refreshes, rejuvenate and detoxifies the YONI!!! It can be Used for addressing nausea, nervous anxiety and constipation. Finally It increases fertility!

Muira puama root (Ptychopetalum ovata): It's also known as Potency wood. Parts used- bark and root. It's a good aphrodisiac tonic, ease stress, nervous exhaustion, fights fatigue. It's useful for treating decreased sex drive and erectile dysfunction (ED). It enhances stamina and psychological function, and soothes upset stomachs. It's also used as a tonic to increases appetite in cases of eating disorders. This herb eases joint pain associated with rheumatism.

Shepherds Purse (Capsella bursa-pastoris): It's a diuretic and uterine stimulant that can be used to help in the retention of water due to its diuretic properties that increases urine output. Shepherds purse has proven to be beneficial for PMS symptoms such as water retention related to the menstrual cycle and reduction of flow during this time. Shepherds purse is deemed useful for all bleeding internal and external. It's useful for treating  excessive menstrual bleeding, nosebleeds, hemorrhoids, dysentery, diarrhea, bleeding of the stomach, kidney, lungs, urinary tract, superficial wounds and scraps. Shepherds purse has anti-inflammatory components that helps it to relieve rheumatism and pain. Traditional Chinese Medicine (TCM) uses Shepherds Purse to clear and brighten vision due to potassium and vitamin C nutrients that's vital for maintaining eye health. Shepherds purse contains a uterus toning agent that contracts the uterus and returns it to normal size after child birth. Poultice can be used for healing superficial wounds and pains in the joints. Cotton swabs soaked in the tincture inserted inside the nostril can stop nosebleeds. The herb is also known for regulating and lowering blood pressure.

Irish Sea Moss (Chondrus crispus): It's a demulcent, expectorant AKA Sea Moss (type of seaweed) and the parts used are the Thallus that's been dried. It has 92 of 102 essential minerals found in the human body and are vital for body functions. It's high in iodine, calcium, bromine and strengthens the digestive system. In Jamaica, it is known as an aphrodisiac and increases libido for men and women. It also increases sperm count and is good at releasing mucus from the body. This herb is an excellent anti-inflammatory herb and makes an excellent addition to holistic treatments. It also acts as a demulcent and expectorant. Irish Sea Moss is an excellent source of bromine, carrageenan, iodine, iron, iodine, magnesium, potassium, vitamin A, B, C, and amino acids. It nourishes on a cellular level that's similar to breast milk in terms of nutritional value. Irish Sea Moss is a Super food and plant base source for thyroid support. It balance hormones, supports and levels detoxification process of kidneys, liver and gut health. It contains roughly 80% mucilage making sea moss suitable for soothing the digestive tract healing conditions such as ulcers and gastritis. It's an excellent respiratory tonic for addressing respiratory issues because of its ability to absorb and expel excess fluid in the lungs that make it useful for bronchitis and pneumonia. Did I forget to mention that Irish Sea Moss is excellent for oral health! It's useful for treating funk breath AKA halitosis! It supports and strengthens teeth and gums for optimal oral health. Irish Sea Moss is also great for smoothies and jellies. It revitalizes the mucus membrane in the body and strengthens cartilage and connective tissue. it also supports joint health due to the anti-inflammatory properties. It contains little to no calories! IT'S ALIVE! It soothes and heals the mucus membrane by promoting release in the body systems for healing. It can be used as a facial cleanser and toner for healing and restoring skin to its natural beauty by healing skin disorders such as acne, blemishes, boils, eczema, irritation, psoriasis, rash, and sunburn.

Stinging Nettle (Urtica Dioica): It's an astringent, diuretic and tonic. Some of its constituents include chlorophyll, formic acid, histamine, iron, and vitamin C. This herb is truly holistic as it supports and strengthens the entire body. It's useful for treating skin condition due to allergies and hay fever. It's also a good treatment option for eczema and as a general tonic and for internal bleeding such as uterine hemorrhage, nosebleeds and anywhere there is hemorrhage. Stinging Nettle can heal urinary dysfunctions such as irritable bladder, painful urination or if you're unable to urinate. It's useful for urinary tract infection (UTI) and urinary inflammation. Urinary problems associated with enlarged prostate (benign prostatic hyperplasia BPH). It's excellent for diabetes mellitus II maintenance due to its hypoglycemic properties that helps level blood sugar. Integrating nettle extract with current therapy is a healthy alternative that supports and heals safely. It's useful as a preventative option for joint pain, signs of aging and hair loss (alopecia). It nourishes and purifies the blood to increase circulation. The herb is high in chlorophyll and nourishes the entire body. It combines well with burdock for eczema treatment.

CRYSTALS FOR HEALING:

Moonstone: Worn as a pendent or placed on the sacral chakra moonstone promotes healing of the reproductive system, increase fertility, decreases premenstrual syndrome symptoms PMS, decrease menstrual pain and balances hormones and emotional stress in females. It's considered a sacred stone with a strong connection to the moon and its cycles. Tuned to the natural feminine mystique, moonstone is an excellent stone for women and great for working with female energy. Moonstone enhances female intuitive abilities by connecting to the goddess power of the earth. It enhances clairvoyance and making those who are unconscious conscious.

Carnelian: Worn as a pendent or placed on the sacral chakra carnelian promotes and increases sexual energy. It promotes healing of female and male reproductive symptoms such as ovaries and testes. It also decreases lower abdominal pain and abdominal pain associated with pregnancy. In combination with the root chakra carnelian is a stone of the universal life force that  promotes releases of toxins in the body, blood purification and promotes absorption of minerals. Carnelian promotes healing by supporting the detox process of the body from drugs and alcohol and other harmful habits. Carnelian promotes energy healing and vitality in the physical body by fostering the ability to focus on our body as a temple, strengthening our awareness to make healthy choices. Carnelian promotes creative energy, courage and leadership skills. Egyptians considered carnelian (biblical reference Odem) to be a sacred stone and worn as an amulet protects from negative energy and increase positive energy.

Pearl Abalone: Also known as 'Mother of pearl' is symbolic of a woman's beauty and purity. It's thought to promote chastity in females while increasing female expression. It has different hues of color that represent our human emotional expressions and changes in life.

Calcite (orange): This stone is symbolic of growth and revitalization. It promotes the flow of sexual and creative energy or that "FIRE"! Calcite has elements of fire that balances, heals and remove blockages from emotional issues related to trauma, depression or past life issues. Calcite removes stagnate energy, reduces mucus and fatigue. It aids in healing the reproductive system, intestinal disorders and gallbladder issues. Whatever the inconvenience, calcite can help remove blockages that keep us from reaching our fullest potential.

Citrine: A good protection stone that revitalizes those who wear it. It purifies and detoxifies the blood while improving concentration, creativity, and imagination! Citrine can be referred to as a "GO GETTER" or "MAKE IT HAPPEN" stone as it heightens will power and sensual/sexual power of both men and women. It enhances mental clarity and brings awareness to conscious and

sub-conscious mind. It heals blood issues, constipation and eases nervous anxiety. This crystal balances hormones and also helps reduce menstrual and PMS symptoms such as hot flashes.

Zincite: It enhances personal power and helps people to embrace sexuality. It also increases fertility, stamina and sexual desire. It removes blockages by stimulating energy so that energy can flow with ease hence furthering the healing process. Zincite eliminates mucus from the body. It's useful for treating menstrual, prostate, PMS and menopause symptoms. It also promotes grounding and increases courage, passion and creativity.

CHAPTER 3

DIGESTIVE SKIN HEALTH (SOLAR PLEXUS CHAKRA)

Our "GO GETTER" attitude the way we see ourselves(self-image) and our spark/fire for life is held in the Solar Plexus or navel chakra. It's represented by a YELLOW orb of electric energy located at the diaphragm just above the navel in our abdomen and is associated with our gut instincts, fight or flight instincts, fear and desires. The stomach, adrenal, pancreas, digestive issues, skin, liver and gallbladder issues are all associated with this chakra. All the toxins created by emotional baggage, rejection, living in the past, shame, lack of power are stored by the liver resulting in the liver dysfunction. This is caused by not flushing toxins properly, hence creating an imbalance. Those who feel FAT or not pretty enough, those who are constantly trying to please the opposite sex and those with eating disorders have all imbalances in this region. ARE YOU NOT COMFORTABLE WITH WHOM YOU ARE? Those in the LGBTQ community living with stereotypes and prejudice everyday can also have imbalances in the Solar Plexus.

HERBS FOR HEALING:

Burdock Root (Arctium lappa): The parts of this herb that are used are its leaves and root. It's an alternative, diuretic, bitter and prebiotic herb. It syncs the bodies systems, creates internal balance and contains high amount of potassium. Traditionally it's used to purify the blood as a liver tonic, to remove toxic waste that accumulates in the blood. It also aids in weight loss and digestion of fats. Burdock root has antioxidant, antibacterial and anti-inflammatory properties that helps with cholesterol levels and lower blood pressure. Its leaves used as a poultice for treating skin disorders such as acne, abscesses, eczema, psoriasis, carbuncles and flakey oily skin. They are also great for skin circulation and skin detoxification. In addition, Burdock is known for its anti-tumor (prevention of breast cancer) properties making it a good herbal remedy for cancer. It's useful for treatment of anorexia nervosa. Burdock is believed to stop cancer cells from metastasizing or spreading to other parts of the body. Burdock relieves joint pain, joint inflammation, and inflammation caused by fibromyalgia, lupus, diabetes and bursitis by removing accumulation and deposits from joints. It's one of the main ingredients in Essiac tea. It combines well with Cleavers, Clovers, Sarsaparilla and Yellow Dock.

Cayenne pepper (Capsicum annuum) AKA African Pepper, African Bird Pepper and/or Red Pepper. It's an anti-inflammatory, anti-septic, carminative, stimulant, sialagogue, and tonic herb. Cayenne pepper is good for relieving gas on the stomach and colic. It helps to reduce stomach pain upset caused by aspirin ingestion. When combined with myrrh, it can be used as an antiseptic gargle to ease cough, soreness and hoarseness in the throat. Cayenne is useful as a fever reducer and anti-inflammatory. It relieves joint pain when applied topically to joints infected with osteoarthritis, sprains, strains and spasms. When applied topically, it may cause a burning sensation. It's helpful in cases of urinary tract inflammation and ear infection due to its anti-inflammatory action. DO NOT GET IN EYES!

Comfrey (Symphytum officinale): AKA Knitbone and it's an anti-inflammatory, astringent, expectorant and demulcent herb that is used for treating hemorrhages and productive cough. It's externally used as a poultice due to its wound and skin healing properties. It's also great for relieving diarrhea, upset stomach, pain reliever and good anti-inflammatory. Comfrey soothes irritated bowels caused by inflammation and promotes healing of gastric disorders such as ulcers. It promotes cell growth or cell proliferation. It's also useful for bone and joint health and can function as a natural healer for broken bones, injury to joints muscles and cartilage.

Life everlasting (Helichrysum stoechas) - promotes good health and longevity of life. It's known for its beauty enhancing abilities as its flower reduces appearance of wrinkles, age spots, dark spots, tightens, tones, and brightens skins appearance. It can be useful for healing cuts, scraps, open wounds, and skin ulcers when applied topically as a poultice. It's also useful for treatment of other ailments such as respiratory conditions. To prepare, boil in a pot of water and inhale the vapors.

Red Clover (Trifolium pratense): The parts of this herb that's used is its flower. It's used as an alternative, antispasmodic, and expectorant herb. It's great for children and adults in treating bronchitis, coughs and whooping cough. It's also helpful for healing chronic skin conditions such as eczema, rosacea, psoriasis, skin cancer, skin sores, diaper rash and skin ulcers (decubitus ulcer). Additional uses of this herb include reducing symptoms of premenstrual syndrome (PMS) such as moodiness, sweats, breast pain (mastalgia), hot flashes and Sexually Transmitted Disease (STD'S). It combines well with Nettles and yellow dock.

Sarsaparilla (Smilax Oofficinalis): It's root is the useful part. It has a high content of iron. It's popular in the United States for how well it nourishes and purifies the blood and cures anemia. Sarsaparilla promotes circulation in the body. It's used as an alternative, anti- rheumatic, diuretic, diaphoretic and tonic herb to relieve symptoms of rheumatism, joint pain and skin problems. Sarsaparilla increases sweating and has been used historically to cure impotency in men. It's been useful for Sexually Transmitted Diseases (STD) such as syphilis and herpes since the 1500's. As a diuretic, sarsaparilla treats urinary infections and reduces infection rate. It's thought to be used by bodybuilders alternatively to steroids due to sarsaparillas ability to build muscle.

Yellow Dock - (Rumex crispus) It's most useful part is its root. It's an alternative, cholagogue, and purgative herb. Yellow Dock is a blood purifier, liver and gallbladder detoxifier. It promotes bile production by purging it downward. This makes Yellow Dock a suitable remedy for constipation as it stimulates the stomach muscles. It removes all kind of stubborn waste from the gastrointestinal tract. It has been used historically for treating chronic skin conditions such as psoriasis, jaundice, skin rashes, and dermatitis (skin inflammation). This herb combines well with burdock, cleavers, and dandelion.

CRYSTALS FOR HEALING:

Amber - It increases warmth and tunes the body to the warm energy of the sun or solar energy. Amber is a high vibration stone that carries the vibration of life. Amber also contain s healing energy that increases innate energy, vitality and strength. It helps to relieve depression and its associated signs and symptoms caused by seasonal disorders. Amber absorbs mental and emotional pain and transforms negative energy. Amber is a good absorption stone making it an excellent stone for women as it absorbs pain, stress and sluggishness that's associated with premenstrual syndrome.

Citrine - It promotes expression and creativity as it synergized and tuned to other stones. Citrine is a manifestation stone. Citrine allows connection to our higher self and helps us accept the divine will. It also promotes metabolism, proper digestion, increases stamina and energy. Citrine is an excellent absorption stone by absorbing pain, stress and sluggishness that's associated with premenstrual syndrome. It balances hormones by reducing hot flashes and fatigue due to PMS.

Copper - Used for its healing properties since the middle age, copper when placed directly on the skin can be an excellent absorption stone. It alleviates pain due to PMS, menstrual pain, arthritis and rheumatism. Copper has a soothing effect on joints and soft tissue. Never use an elixir! Copper also promotes concentration in adults and children. It enhances the detoxification process by stimulating the stomach, liver and pancreas.

CHAPTER 4
BLOOD, CARDIOVASCULAR, RESPIRATORY/CHEST HEALTH (HEART CHAKRA)

Our emotional, spiritual, mental, and physical well-being is all part of our heart chakra. It's located in the center of the chest at the sternum and is represented by a GREEN orb of electric energy. This is associated with love of family and friends, forgiveness, romance and compassion. If you find yourself stuck in the past, reliving childhood issues, not committed, unforgiving, and not trustful of others, then you have imbalances in your heart chakra. Those who are still bitter about relationships that didn't end well or in divorce and those who are still harboring hate for their ex-spouse or significant other are letting them live rent free in their heart, mind, body, and soul; Without forgiveness all have imbalances here in this region. Some health issues found in this area include cardiovascular issues, high blood pressure, hemorrhage, immune disorders, circulatory issues, heart conditions, respiration issues, allergies, and anxiety induced palpations.

HERBS FOR HEALING:

Chaparral (Larrea divaricata): It nourishes and purifies the blood, and cleanses the lymphatic system with its Anti-inflammatory, antineoplastic, antioxidant and diuretic properties. This herb is helpful for respiratory issues associated with the common cold. It's a great treatment option for snakebites. Chaparral strengthens the immune system ridding the body of parasites, chickenpox, menstrual cramps, and skin disorders.

Lilly of the Valley (Convallaria majalis): It's a cardioactive, diuretic, tonic and purgative herb that's highly esteemed and desirable as a herbal remedy for cardiac concerns. The action of the herb closely emulates Digitalis, although it's not as intense. It strengthens weak, tired and irritable hearts while nourishing cardiac muscles, cells, and blood. It also reduces swelling in limbs associated with heart issues and useful for congestive heart failure. It can be mixed well with Hawthorn and Motherwort.

Motherwort (Leonurus cardiaca): It's an antispasmodic, cardiac tonic sedative with mild anti-tumor abilities. It's known to strengthen heartbeats and can be useful for cardiac conditions that are associated with anxiety and rapid heartbeat (tachycardia). It's useful for treating uterine conditions, absent, suppressed, delayed menstrual cycle and also reduces menstrual cramps. It calms nervous energy and hyperactive thyroid.

Milk Thistle (Silybum marianum) Parts of it that are used are the seeds. Milk thistle is a cholagogue, demulcent, and galactagogue herb. There is folk medicine beliefs that say the white marks on the leaves are Virgin Mary's spilled breast milk. As the name suggests, milk thistle safely enhances the secretion of mother's breast milk. Traditionally, it's used to treat malaria. In addition, milk thistle promotes bile production and secretions from the gallbladder and liver. It's used in the treatment of alcoholism, cirrhosis, hepatitis, liver poisoning and mushroom poisoning. it mixes well with burdock root and dandelion.

Prickly Ash Bark (Zanthoxylum americanum): It's useful parts are the berries and bark. It's an alternative, carminative, diaphoretic, and tonic herb that promotes circulation. It provides temporary relief that reduces pain caused by illness and disorders such as sickle cell, abdominal disorders, rheumatism, arthritis, gallbladder disease and intestinal spasms. it also helps to treat varicose veins and hemorrhoids, however it may be slow in action. DO NOT USE DURING PREGNANCY! It kills bacteria, parasites and can be applied topically to treat skin conditions and scabies.

Yellow Dock (Rumex crispus): It's a blood purifier, detoxifier and promotes bile production. It's useful for constipation and helps digestive issues particularly of fats. It's filled with antioxidants that fights free radicals. It can be applied topically to reduce swelling and inflammation. It also reduces swelling of respiratory tract and related issues. It's

been known among herbalist to cool liver heat. Yellow Dock is thought to cure "bad blood" or issues of the blood such as anemia. The leaves can be used as poultice to be applied topically or as salve ointment.

CRYSTALS FOR HEALING:

Aventurine - Green aventurine is a prosperity stone that promotes luck in relationships and employment, not just monetary prosperity. It also increases humor and confidence. Green aventurine promotes grounding, anchoring, optimism and balance of emotions. This attributes and more make it an excellent stone for love

and relationships. It helps you to release attachments in order to move forward. it increases circulation, eases heart and circulatory issues, and regenerates cells It's good for improving vitality, and our universal life force or "chi". It dispels negative energy, reduces stress and anxiety, lowers blood pressure and relieves skin irritation due to its anti-inflammatory properties.

Jade - This crystal dispels negative energy, dissolves blockages, and promotes harmony in love, life, and finances. Jade stimulates the kidneys and gallbladder having and has a

detoxifying effect on the body. Jade enhances emotional harmony while instilling calmness and easing stress to those who wear it. Jade grants insightful dreams when placed or worn as an amulet. Jade is considered a good luck charm or sacred stone that symbolizes compassion, modesty, and wisdom. The Chinese considers Jade a medicinal stone that's used to strengthen the heart, lungs, blood and bones.

Malachite - A stone known for relieving lovesickness, heartache and pain, malachite promotes balance and harmony of the heart chakra, clearing a way for undying love. Malachite is a stone that eliminate chest pains, cardiac issues and helps with concentration. Malachite also promotes spiritual understanding, breaks old psych, mental and emotional connections, and severs negative connections and patterns. Malachite increases circulation of blood

in the heart while resonating harmonious vibrations. It's believed to be a stone of protection from the evil eye, and that it heightens your intuition /"radar". Early Egyptians used malachite in powdered form as eye shadow.

Rose Quartz - It enhances love and desires of the heart and transmits vibes of unconditional love. Rose quartz decreases aggression and aggravating conditions. When placed on the chest, rose quartz can ease anxiety and stress related conditions. Rose quartz balances our emotional center and make it easy to deal with matters of the heart and relationships. Rose quartz gives off only love vibrations.

Rose Quartz Water Mist

You can create a refreshing mist of rose water by simply boiling rose petals using distilled water:

- Pull the rose petals from rose
- Make- 1 cup
- Rinse the petals
- Discard the stem
- Boil petals using distilled water (2 cups in a pan) or pour boiling water OVER the petals in the pan
- Let it simmer for 45 minutes
- Let it cool completely
- Strain contents into bottle or container
- Keep refrigerated until use. Water will last about a week in refrigerator

CHAPTER 5
THROAT & GLAND HEALTH (THROAT CHAKRA)

Our endocrine system is related to our throat chakra. All our communications and expression are associated with our throat chakra. It's located at the center or base of the throat represented by a BLUE orb of electric energy. Ailments like sore throat, laryngitis, thyroid issues, persistent cough, ear infections, teeth and gums are associated with the throat chakra, it is connected to our mental function. People who are dealing with verbal abuse, the inability to speak up for themselves, or those who do too much talking and not enough listening have imbalances in this region. Also, those who have repressed anger, pure frustration due to lack of frequent expression may have an unbalanced throat chakra.

HERBS FOR HEALING:

Bladderwrack (Fucus Vesiculosus). Common name: Kelp. It's an anti- hypothyroid, anti-rheumatic herb. As an original source of iodine, it's rich in iodine, and also bromine, alginic acid, mannitol, carotene, zeaxanthin, and potassium. This herb is commonly used for the treatment of goiter and hypothyroid or underactive thyroid. It also heals associated signs and symptoms such as overweight and obesity by regulating the thyroid function and iron deficiency. Bladderwrack boosts metabolism and its useful for relieving joint pain in conditions such as arthritis and rheumatism. it's useful in reducing the effects of arteriosclerosis (hardening of the arteries). Topical application to the joints has been known to relieve joint pain. Topical application to the skin aids skin disease, skin eruptions, insect bites, cellulite and overall skin health. It's useful in treatment of urinary bladder infections and guards against blood clots. it's helpful in maintaining blood sugar levels and controlling LDL or (bad cholesterol). It contains fucoidan which is an anti-tumor property it uses to stop unwanted cell growth. Helps improve and maintain digestive health, aids weight loss.

Cleavers (Garlium aparine) The aerial parts are the useful parts. It's an alternative, anti-inflammatory, antineoplastic, diaphoretic, diuretic and tonic herb that's useful treatment for lymphadenitis or swollen glands in parts of the body particularly adenoid and tonsils. It heals urinary and gastric conditions. It's historic for treating tumors and ulcers and also useful for skin conditions such as psoriasis and lymphatic drainage. It combines well with Burdock, Yellow Dock and Pokeweed.

Elderberry (Sambucus nigra**):** The parts used include- Bark, leaves, berries and flowers. It's a purgative, diuretic, expectorant and laxative natural herb. Elderberry supports the immune system and can be used for relieving cold, fevers, hay fever (allergic rhinitis) influenza, H1N1 swine flu, and sinusitis. Did I mention Elderberry supports and boost the immune system?! It's great at addressing respiratory symptoms such as bronchitis, coughs, and asthma. There are no side effects compared to over the counter and prescription drugs.

DIY Elderberry Cough Syrup:
- Mash up 1 cup of dried organic elderberries or fresh elderberry
- Add a few slices of ginger or 2 tablespoons of ginger root powder
- Add 3 1/2 cups of spring water
- Add 3/4 cups of raw agave or honey (add this ingredient last)
- Add elderberries and ginger to boiling water
- Reduce heat to low, and let it simmer for 1 hour or until half the water is evaporated
- Let it sit for 15 minutes, and cool, then strain into jar
- Discard remaining elderberries and ingredients
- Finally, add some raw agave or honey
- Take 1 tablespoon every day

You can store it for up to 3 months in refrigerator. Do not give to children under the age of 1 year if using honey.

CHAPTER 6

EARS, VISION, NEUROLOGICAL DISORDERS HEALTH (BROW CHAKRA)

Our mind's eye, intuition, psychic abilities, dreams, and intention are all connected with our brow chakra or third-eye. It's located at the center of the forehead, just above the eyebrows and is represented by an INDIGO orb of electric energy. The brow chakra is directly connected to our spiritual eyesight. It's responsible for how we are guided intuitively. An unbalanced brow chakra can cause symptoms such as difficult learning, ears, nose and throat (ENT) problems. This can also cause vision problems such as glaucoma, blindness, dyslexia, farsighted, nearsighted and eye styles. It also causes ear problems such as deafness or ringing in the ears, ear pain, tension headaches, dizziness, nervousness, hallucinations and fainting. If you have an imbalanced brow chakra, you may also have difficulty interpreting dreams. For a moment, let's pretend your child suffer from some of these conditions, and now, the disease is manifesting itself into learning difficulties. These are some herbs for balancing the brow or third-eye.

HERBS FOR HEALING:

Eyebright (Euphrasia officinalis) It's aerial parts used. It's an anti-inflammatory, anti-catarrhal, astringent herb. As the name suggest, it's most commonly used to treat eye conditions that are age related vision problems like blepharitis, cataracts conjunctivitis (pink eye), light sensitivity, eye stinging, tearful eyes, inflamed blood shot or strained eyes. It's useful as a topical compress for eyes. In addition, the anti-catarrhal property in Eyebright make it great for relieving sinuses, nasal congestion, chest congestion, allergies, cold and flu related issues by reducing mucus in the mucus membrane. Eyebright is also used for skin conditions such as acne by removing oil and tightening the pores.

Kava Kava (Piper methysticum): Its root is its useful part. Kava Kava induces mental clarity and relaxation while relieving dizziness, depression, joint pain, musculoskeletal pain, menopause symptoms, nervous exhaustion, anxiety, insomnia caused by anxiety, phobias, restlessness and stress. In addition kava kava can be used for curing urinary tract infections, urinary inflammation and cystitis. Kava Kava is not addictive but do not take with alcohol. The same goes for over the counter medications or prescription medications.

Pennywort (Umbilicus rupestris): anti-anodyne, demulcent. It's good for treating earache safely and effectively in children. It can soothe tooth pain due to its anti-anodyne pain relieving properties. Because of its antibiotic properties, Pennywort accelerates wound healing process, lowers fever and increases memory. Pennywort can be eaten raw or used as a tea to increase  alertness and promote increased brain function. Pennyworts soothing ability on the central nervous system decreases symptoms of attention deficit disorder ADD, senile dementia and increase sleep function due to stress and mental fatigue.

 **Red Sage** (Salvia officinalis): It's an antiseptic, astringent and carminative herb that's great for treating mouth and throat disorders such as inflammation of the tongue, gums, tonsils, laryngitis, pharyngitis and it soothes mucus membranes and can function as a mouthwash and gargle.

Chamomile (Anthemus nobile): It's an antispasmodic, anti-tumor, carminative, sedative, anti-inflammatory and analgesic herb that's safe and effective for children use. Most commonly, it is used to ease stress related issues. Chamomile gives a calming effect that's useful for combating attention deficit disorder (ADD), anxiety, irritability, restlessness, and insomnia. It has carminative properties that help to relieve  gas or flatulence, and related gas pain. It combines well with ginger for alleviating morning sickness. Chamomile creates a soothing effect on the digestive tract that heals peptic ulcers. It soothes and relaxes tense muscles caused by premenstrual syndrome pain (PMS). The Apigenin molecule found in chamomile has the potential to prevent endometrial cancer cells from spreading to new areas.

CRYSTALS FOR HEALING:

Angelite: It decreases negative energy, anger, anxiety and stress, while increasing emotional stability bringing balance, a sense of security and love. Angelite creates a divine spiritual connection that increases all communication types as well as with angels and spirit guides. It also helps with feelings of grief by giving increased strength to cope with illness and death. It's a good stone for increasing loving angelic guidance.

Lapis: It helps to speak your truth and speak up for yourself. Lapis guides you to connect to your inner truth and power by promoting honest and clear communications. Lapis enhances increased connections mentally and spiritually allowing you to focus and tune into the un-seen hence developing a more intellectual awareness. Lapis lazuli thought to be a master healer stone is useful for throat, thyroid, larynx and vocal cord issues while cleansing the immune system and thymus gland. It reduces swollen glands, inflammation and useful for eyes, ears and nasal issues ENT. When placed on the brow and throat, lapis promotes balance, removes blockages and increases intuition. It also improves learning and memory.

Sodalite: It's the stone of communication and learning sometimes called the "poets stone" and it promotes logical thinking. Sodalite filters negative communication by increasing your power to speak and be conscious of your thought process. In addition, it eases stress and anxiety, and improves blood pressure. Sodalite promotes and stimulates absorption of fluids. When worn sodalite is aid to increase musical talents, improve meditation, regulate the thyroid and glandular functions by cleansing; the white veins are indicative of this belief. Sodalite is useful for throat issues such as hoarseness, throat irritation and vocal cord issues. In addition, it can be used as a substitute to lapis.

Turquoise: This crystal improves communication and is considered a stone of protection when worn as an amulet. It is considered a healing stone with good detox properties, by American Indians. Turquoise helps to relieve throat and lung issues. It's also useful in relieving joint pain caused by gout and rheumatism. In addition, folklore considers turquoise a stone of beauty.

CHAPTER 7

EMOTIONAL, MENTAL, NEUROLOGICAL HEALTH (CROWN CHAKRA)

Our crown chakra connects us with God. It's is where we get our divine wisdom and how we connect with the universe. This region is where we conjure faith and connect with the universal flow of energy, or religious views. Here is where we become enlightened beings. The crown chakra is the center that integrates energy with all the other chakras. It's located at the top of the head/crown and is represented by a PURPLE orb of energy that affects the central nervous system. A person without religious beliefs or, belief in a higher universal power, or a person with loss of faith has an unbalanced crown chakra. Depression, feeling lost without sense of purpose, dementia, schizophrenia, epilepsy, Parkinson's, paralysis, multiple sclerosis, senile dementia, amnesia, Alzheimer, immune system deficiency and, insomnia are related to imbalances of the crown chakras.

HERBS FOR HEALING:

Jamaican Dogwood (Piscidia erythrina): Its useful parts are the bark and stem. It is an Anodyne, antispasmodic and sedative herb that's used in Central America as a fish poison. It's powerful and extremely effective for healing anxiety, body pain, dysmenorrhea or painful menstrual, headache, hysteria, insomnia, migraine and neuralgia pain caused by sciatica. You can crush its leaves and apply them to the head to ease your headaches. You can also crush them and apply to joints to relieve pain. Although it's nonpoisonous to humans, it's advised that you consult with your doctor before using it.

Kava Kava Root (Piper methysticum): it's an analgesic, euphoriant and sedative natural herb that acts on receptors in the brain making it useful for treating anxiety, Attention deficit hyperactivity disorder (ADHD), depression, insomnia, stress, restlessness, and other social phobias. In addition Kava Kava Root can be used to treat urinary tract infections (UTI) due to its anti-inflammatory and antiseptic properties.

Kola Nut (Cola vera): It's an antidepressant, astringent and a stimulant herb. It is mostly used by Nigerians and is considered to be highly medicinal. It increases oxygen flow and circulation, improves concentration, alertness, and promotes healthy organs in both men and women. It's also useful for combating depression. It's also one of the many ingredients found in cola and energy drinks.

Lady Slipper (cypripedium pubescens): It's an antispasmodic, hypnotic, sedative and nervine herb. It inhibits stress related symptoms and reactions such as headaches and epilepsy. It enhances your mood that may have been brought by depression. This herb reduces nerve pain, and heals neuralgia nerve pain, hallucinations, insomnia, and hysteria. In addition, it reduces heat by sweat absorption and regulates body temperature.

Lavender (lavendula officinalis): This herb is an antidepressant, antispasmodic and a carminative, all at the same time. It's also a mood enhancer that reduces anxiety and stress. It's useful for stress related headaches, combating depression and nervous exhaustion. Lavender is a natural sleep enhancer. In addition, it aids digestion, remedies gas, cures insomnia and acne, heals burns, headache and treats hair loss. It mixes well with Valerian and lady slipper.

Lemon Balm (Melissa officinalis): it's an antibacterial, carminative and sedative herb that supports mental and emotional health by fighting anxiety, fear, hysteria, headaches and insomnia. It inhibits nervousness, high blood pressure and melancholia or severe sadness. It also eases tension caused by attention deficit disorder.

Passion Flower (Passiflora incarnata): It's an antispasmodic, anodyne, hypnotic and sedative plant. It's most commonly used to eliminate nervousness and insomnia by promoting restful sleep. It's useful in extreme cases of anxiety and it relieves seizures, Parkinson's disease, muscle spasms, involuntary contractions and other pain inducing conditions. It also relaxes heart arteries and lowers blood pressure. In addition, it can help with addiction by reducing withdrawal symptoms from alcohol and drug abuse. It combines well with Hop, Jamaican Dogwood, and Valerian.

Blue Vervain (Verbena hastata): it's a nervine and sedative herb that's commonly used to fight depression due to its calming effect. It promotes relaxation and eases tension while eliminating mood swings and stress. It's useful for pain relief due to the numbing or sedative effect it has on the nerves. It's useful for joint pain and

inflammation such as arthritis and gout. In addition, it helps with premenstrual syndrome (PMS), abdominal cramping and bloating. It heals respiratory disorders such as cough, chest congestion and bronchitis.

CRYSTALS FOR HEALING:

Agate Purple - A stone of intuition, Agate strengthens spiritual enlightenment and development. Agate is known for bringing balance and clarity of thoughts, vision and insight. Agate relieves headaches, dizziness, vertigo, eye pain and inflammation. In addition it deals with skin problems such as acne, boils, blemishes and irritation. It's considered a good protector stone due to its high vibration that repels negativity.

Amethyst - It's considered a master healer and stone of protection. Amethyst is known to make unconscious, conscious. It enhances peaceful sleep and mental clarity. Folklore says it protects against evil eye magic, nightmares, negativity and drunkenness. When placed in a room amethyst clears negativity and protects the home form burglars. When placed at the crown chakra amethyst improves any kind of mediation.

Lepidolite - Considered to be a healing stone, lepidolite eases and balances emotional issues by inhibiting feelings of anxiety, anger, addiction, stress, post-traumatic stress disorder PTSD, panic attacks, and depression. Lepidolite is thought to reconstruct DNA. It increases peaceful interactions with others through speech and all other forms of communication. Lepidolite clears blockages promoting better meditation and balances heart chakra. When placed or worn on the body lepidolite vibrates and heals all kinds of the dis-eases in that area.

Sugilite - It promotes a calming effect on the nervous system and protects from negativity. Folklore thought tells that sugilite gives off warnings of the end of the world. It's very useful for children who are having a hard time adjusting at school or learning in general. Sugilite promotes good behavior and reactions to uncomfortable situations.

ABOUT THE AUTHOR

Liz Christian is the founder of Touch by Liz alternative and holistic services. Degreed in the art of Complementary and Alternative Medicine Ms. Christian has an appreciation for herbs, crystals, relaxation massage, energy work, and healing touch modalities. She regularly contributes her time guiding adults, children and seniors through alternative healing approaches and natural cures. After years of direct and indirect use of alternative treatments, she decided that she would save the world one person at a time.

(Please note: Information in this book IS NOT a substitute for consulting a health care professional. All information contained in this book, including information relating to medical and health conditions, products and treatments, is for informational purposes only. Please consult your doctor or health care professional before starting any alternative treatments, diets, supplements or exercise programs.)

Printed in the United States
By Bookmasters